37 Secrets About
Prosperity

"A revealing look at how you manifest wealth."

By Randy Gage

Gage, Randy.
    37 secrets about prosperity / by Randy Gage.
    — 1st ed.
    p. cm.
    Thirty-seven secrets about your prosperity
    "A revealing look at how you manifest wealth."
    LCCN 2003102894
    ISBN 0971557888

    1. Success—Psychological aspects. 2. Success in
business. 3. Finance, Personal.   I. Title.
II. Title: Thirty-seven secrets about your prosperity

BF637.S8G34 2003   158.1
                              QBI33-1267

Introduction

Prosperity is a funny thing. Everybody knows the word, but few people understand what it really means. Fewer still know the secrets it takes to unlock it in your life. But once you learn these secrets, it's a bold new world. Health, happiness and wealth do funny things to a person. They let you start each day with joy and dynamic energy; they let you close each day with peace and harmony; and they let you live each day with adventure.

I've been very blessed to uncover these prosperity secrets and discover my real assignment in life—which is to share them with you. Now, I move the responsibility on to you.

It's your turn now. Someone close to you needs this information. So now the next adventure is yours . . .

On the journey,

Randy Gage
Hollywood, Florida
March 2003

ഗ 1 ഇ

YOU CAN'T OUT GIVE
THE UNIVERSE.

This is the first fundamental secret of prosperity, and one that so many people miss. They approach prosperity as a "give me" thing, and never tune in to the real energy that surrounds it.

Everything in the universe is based on the principle of trading value for value. But it is an unbalanced scale. What you send out comes back to you in multiples. Usually tenfold. So, when you sow seeds of good, much more good will come back to you.

This holds true for the money you tithe, the love you give, and the good you do. As hard as you may try, you can't out give the universe.

So go out and make a random act of kindness, sow a seed to someone in need, and be extra nice to that clerk in the checkout line. Much more prosperity is coming your way!

‹ 2 ›

THE ONLY FREE CHEESE IS
IN THE MOUSETRAP.

That statement sounds like I'm being flippant, but it actually is a very concise, and very profound summary of how the laws of prosperity operate.

You don't get rich winning the lottery, getting an inheritance, or discovering oil in your backyard. Those things may happen to poor people and create some temporary wealth. But the wealth won't stay around, or you won't achieve true prosperity for free. There is always a price to pay: the fair exchange of values we discussed in the first secret.

A big part of the price you pay to become prosperous is becoming the kind of person that handles prosperity responsibly. Studies have shown again and again that most poor people who win large windfalls in the lottery are broke and miserable ten years later. And we are talking about people who have won ten, twenty, or even forty million dollars! They got the cash, but they didn't have the prosperity consciousness. So the money never stayed, and the other elements of prosperity never showed up.

Nothing comes for free. If you let the clerk give you the extra $5 by mistake, you find a way to wire your house for cable without paying for it, or you help yourself to an extra newspaper when no one is looking—you are incurring a definite karma debt. And those debts always come due. Prosperous people never look for anything for free. They are always happy to exchange value for everything.

ೞ 3 ೞ

PROSPEROUS PEOPLE ARE NOT OVERLY RELIGIOUS PEOPLE.

While prosperous people are not necessarily religious people, they are deeply spiritual. They understand that obsessing over dogmas and doctrines takes them further away from their true nature. There is elegant simplicity in the pathway of prosperity from vision to manifestation. And true prosperity is inclusive, not exclusive.

☙ **4** ❧

WEALTH DOESN'T HAPPEN TO YOU. YOU HAPPEN TO WEALTH.

Yes, you may read about the occasional person who inherits great wealth or wins a bundle at the horse track. But true wealth—the kind that stays with you—comes as a result of a very deliberate process. It doesn't happen "to" you. You happen to it.

You become a wealthy person in your mind; then ,you manifest it on the physical plane by becoming the kind of person that attracts prosperity to you.

෬ 5 ෩

YOU BUILD YOUR PROSPERITY
WITH WORDS.

Or more specifically, the words you speak. It always amazes me when people affirm the most negative things. A friend called me today to say that he had backed his truck into a tree. He told me, "Every time things really start going good for me, something always happens to set me back." Well of course it does, he's programming that belief right into his subconscious mind, which orders it to take place on the physical realm.

Think how many times good things happen and people say something like, "I can't believe it! I never win anything." Then something bad happens. They drop a dish, spill something or get stood up, and they proclaim, "I knew that was going to happen!" Of course they did.

I hear people say things like, "Every winter I get at least three colds." I used to say, "About once a year, my back goes out." And of course it did. 'Til I stopped affirming that. Hasn't happened now in over nine years.

Some people think it's polite or a good way to fit in by speaking of themselves in demeaning terms. Statements like, "I'm always a day late and a dollar short," will endear you to broke people. But they also repel prosperity and become self-fulfilling prophecies. So if you're going to determine your prosperity by the words you speak, why not affirm things like the positive statement below?

"Money is attracted to me like a magnet!"

ങ **6** ൠ

HEALTH, LOVE, HAPPINESS, AND MONEY ARE INFINITE.

If you give someone a hug, does that reduce the number of hugs you have left to give? Of course not. In fact, if you are known as the kind of person who gives hugs, you will likely attract a lot more of them to you.

Things that make up true prosperity like health, love, happiness, and money are infinite, and actually create their own expansion.

The more love you give away, the more you attract to you. Abundant health builds upon itself and fosters more. Happiness operates in the same way. Because you can't out give the universe, money that you circulate creates its own energy, which creates ripple effects of prosperity, which ultimately find their way back to you. It is a self-replicating cycle that goes on indefinitely.

‹ 7 ›

Prosperity Operates on the Vacuum Principle.

Nature abhors a vacuum, and will always fill it with good. The universe cannot place something in your hand, if it is clenched around something else. The best way to attract something positive is to release something negative, and create a vacuum for good.

If you want some new clothes, best to clean out your closet first, and donate some old clothes to the homeless shelter. If you are looking for your soul mate, you must first let go of any abusive other relationship you are in. When you are not attracting all the prosperity you are seeking in your life, ask yourself what you are holding on to that you should be releasing.

C8 **8** BO

POOR PEOPLE OBSESS ABOUT MONEY THE MOST.

There is a lot of talk among the middle and lower class about how fixated rich people are about money. Many of them believe that the rich only think about money. Nothing could be further from the truth. In fact, poor people think about money a whole lot more than rich people do.

This is a case of what psychologists call "projecting." Meaning that people project their own fears, prejudices, and motives on others.

By their very nature, poor people think about money all the time. I remember when I was broke, it was about all I could think about. If the phone rang, I wondered if it was a bill collector. When I drove somewhere, I worried whether my car would break down and I wouldn't be able to afford fixing it. I noticed people with nice cars and clothes and I was jealous of them. I wondered what they did to deserve what they had.

I was always juggling bills, making payment arrangements and wondering how I would pay the next round. I was fixated with money, because everything bad that was happening to me seemed to be a result of not having enough money.

Now that I have money, I very seldom think about it. Money is one of the lubricants that enhance life and magnify the experiences you have. Once you "get the money thing out of the way," it allows you to experience the benefits without the anxiety.

❦ 9 ❧

YOU MAY ASK FOR WHAT YOU THINK YOU WANT. BUT YOU WILL GET WHAT YOU REALLY WANT.

When I pray for others, and myself, rather than ask for specific things, I always ask for the highest good. If you seek something specific, better to ask for it "or something better."

As a child, I thought I loved shrimp. Once I grew up, I figured out that I like shrimp, but what I really love is cocktail sauce. Many times we let past events, emotional baggage and other things cloud our judgment. We think we want one thing, but often what we really want is something different. This can be good or bad.

For the first 30 years of my life, I thought I wanted to be a millionaire. In reality, what I really wanted was to be a victim, and get sympathy from those around me. It was only when what I really wanted changed from being a victim to being a millionaire that it actually happened.

ℭ **10** ℬ

THE MOST POWERFUL TOOL FOR PROSPERITY IS WISDOM.

If a fool and his money are soon parted (and they are), it stands to reason that a wise man or woman will soon attract their prosperity to them. And they do.

If you want great wealth, seek first uncommon wisdom.

☙ **11** ❧

PROSPERITY IS YOUR BIRTHRIGHT, AND NATURAL CONDITION.

When we are unhealthy, unhappy or poor, it is because we strayed from our path, and lost contact with our true nature.

Your natural state is health. It is only when you are out of sync that disease enters your body. You came into this realm as a happy person. Unhappiness is a conscious choice, requiring you to make that decision. Unhappiness is not natural, and it is not healthy.

Likewise, you were born to be rich. Struggling for existence is not noble, not natural, and not necessary. When you live your life by the universal laws of prosperity, wealth comes to you as naturally as rain waters the flowers.

03 **12** 80

PROSPERITY IS MANIFESTED FROM THE ETHERS AROUND YOU.

The universe has provided for all of your needs. Prosperity is in the ethers all around you. Like a soldier waiting for orders, prosperity stands on guard, waiting to be called forth.

The mediums that man uses to manifest prosperity from the ethers onto the physical plane are IDEAS.

০঵ **13** ৵০

ONCE YOU DISCOVER YOUR ASSIGNMENT, PROSPERITY WILL DISCOVER YOU.

Once you begin doing the work you are truly meant to do, the universe will reward you with good. This is the way universal laws work, with no exception.

When you do your assignment, you attack it with passion, zeal and dedication. And, because you come with that mindset, you perform at an extraordinary level, attracting extraordinary results.

All people are subconsciously searching for their "jihad." A cause, movement or vision that is greater than they are. When you are on your assignment, people sense this power and want to be a part of it. You attract powerful people who share their prosperity with you.

෬ 14 ෩

WHEN YOU HAVE A POWERFUL VISION, YOU BEND THE UNIVERSE TO YOUR WILL.

This is one of those things that the uninitiated have a hard time understanding, and especially believing. But at its ultimate level, EVERYTHING in the universe can be distilled down to an energy vibration. And energy vibrations can certainly be aware of, and respond to, other energy vibrations.

So, yes, you really can attract prosperity to you, just as you can manifest a parking space, an elevator coming, or a hotel room available.

When you have a compelling dream and a strong belief in that dream, you attract partners, manifest resources, impact markets, and create an entire roller coaster of reactions to your vision.

☙ **15** ❧

YOUR PROSPERITY WILL BE THE AVERAGE OF THE PROSPERITY OF YOUR FIVE CLOSEST FRIENDS.

This one is so predictable it is amazing to the uninitiated. Take the five people who are closest to you in your life; add up their yearly income from last year and divide it by five, to see what your annual salary will be this year.

And it doesn't just work for money . . .

This is operating within several prosperity laws, and holds true in all areas. Look at the relationships, health, and happiness of those closest to you, and you'll find that you are right in the middle.

෨ **16** ෯

FAITH DRAWS YOUR PROSPERITY FROM THE STOREHOUSE.

We know that ideas are the conduits that allow man to transform prosperity from the ethers into manifestation on the physical realm. But it won't happen without belief as well.

You must see your good, seek your good, and believe in your good to make it appear. Those with less talent, but stronger belief, achieve far more, far sooner, than those with ability, but little faith.

❦ **17** ❧

PROSPERITY CANNOT EXIST WITHOUT MONEY.

If you are prosperous, you are:

1) Healthy
2) Happy
3) Rich

Two out of three ain't bad. But it ain't prosperity either. True prosperity takes all three.

Some rich people are sick, bitter and lonely. They are not prosperous. By the same token, if you are healthy, spiritually grounded, and have a great marriage, but struggle to pay your credit cards each month—you are certainly not prosperous either. Prosperity is all encompassing.

❧ 18 ❧

WHAT OTHER PEOPLE CALL CHALLENGES ARE THE CHARACTER-BUILDERS THAT BRING YOU PROSPERITY.

It's not that prosperity is meant to be elusive or difficult. It is not. But it only comes to those who are on the proper path, and who have become the kind of person that is equal to prosperity.

A big part of the process for most people is experiencing the necessary challenges to shape their character, and develop their wisdom. You gain wisdom from the mistakes of others, and your own mistakes. The more you learn from the examples of others, the fewer mistakes of your own are necessary. But all of us have some lessons that we must learn.

Prosperity-conscious individuals understand this, and welcome those challenges as the stepping-stones they must ascend; in order to become the person they need to be.

⋄ **19** ⋄

THE UNIVERSE ALWAYS GETS ITS TITHE.

You can tithe joyfully, lovingly and gratefully to the source of your spiritual nourishment. Or you can have it taken from you involuntarily at the transmission shop, doctor's office, or courthouse. But the universe will always get its tithe, just as the tides will rise and fall.

‹ **20** ›

YOUR DREAM MUST BE AS BIG AS YOU ARE.

It doesn't serve you or the Universe to play small. Humility is a virtue, but false modesty or holding back from your highest good is anti-prosperity. Muscles that aren't exercised atrophy, and dreams, vision and desires do the same.

Your vision of your future must be bold, daring and imaginative, if you want it to manifest. You need the compelling "pull" that a big dream will exert upon you. It must be so powerful that you throw the sheets off in the morning and race into your day with anticipation.

C8 **21** 80

PROSPERITY LEAVES CLUES.

Truly prosperous people are easy to spot. They make their bed in the morning; they have a clean desk; and they even wash their rental car. They do these things not because they have to, but because they want to, in order to be in a prosperous environment.

They treat the toll-taker, waitress, and cashier with the same kindness as they would show a Head of State. They respect their own body, and treat it accordingly.

෫ **22** ෨

VISION BRINGS YOUR PROSPERITY TO YOU MUCH SOONER.

Prosperity is manifested in the mind first. You can stumble across random blessings, but true and boundless prosperity comes as a result of envisioning it first.

From the time I put the things I was seeking on my Dream board, it took me about two years to manifest all of them. I honestly believe that if I had not done that—it would have taken me at least ten years to get the same results.

Affirmations, goal cards, and other devices that enhance and strengthen your vision have the same result. You actually program your subconscious mind with the desired goal. And once something is programmed in your subconscious, it has to happen.

❧ 23 ❧

Prosperity has Nothing to do with Opportunities, Chance, or Luck.

The masses think prosperity comes as a result of special opportunities, random chances, or lucky events. This is true, but only in the sense that you create those opportunities.

Even education, training, and skills are not as important as your consciousness and beliefs. Because it is your consciousness and beliefs, that drive your education, training and skills.

༖ **24** ༺

PROSPERITY IS NOT AN ABUNDANCE OF THINGS. IT IS A MINDSET.

Sports cars, mansions and money do not create prosperity.
They are symptoms of it. True prosperity is a mindset in
the recipient.

Likewise, the absence of money, possessions and other things is
not poverty. Their absence is a condition of the poverty
situation. Poverty itself is simply a mindset.

ᚈ **25** ᚉ

YOUR MIND IS AN INSTRUMENT FOR POVERTY OR PROSPERITY.

This is either the scariest thing you will ever hear, or the most liberating insight you will ever learn. Make it the latter, and you are well on your way to abundance.

No two people ever view the same event in the same way. Where one may see a threat, the other sees opportunity. Suppose you are offered a chance to participate in a business opportunity. You could approach this in a number of different ways.

You could jump in blindly, without doing any research, just because you are enamored with the idea of getting rich. You could enter a very bad situation and lose a lot of money.

Or, scenario two, you could figure that any deal you find out about is already too late. You could figure the "insiders" get all the sweetheart deals and it's probably much too good to be true. So you pass up the chance to buy IBM when it is $10 a share.

Another scenario occurs when you get offered a situation; you have confidence in yourself; you study it thoroughly; and, you make a sound decision. How you will react to it is determined almost entirely by your mindset. What you expect in life. Of all the tools you can use to manifest your prosperity, your mind is the most powerful.

◌ **26** ◌

SELFISHNESS IS NECESSARY FOR TRUE PROSPERITY.

In fact, selfishness is your moral prerogative.

Most people will tell you that your moral imperative is to put the interests of the many before the interests of the one. That you should sacrifice yourself for the "greater good."

This idea is very dangerous to your self-esteem, your prosperity and your life. Relinquishing your happiness for the sake of others, known or unknown, verifies, to yourself and others, that you are small and unworthy of even your own attention. It's actually anti-humanity, and it makes you mentally ill.

Your survival and your pursuit of happiness must form the foundation of your value system.

To make your life, by your own means, toward your own standards, and for your own enjoyment. Anything less than that is harmful to you. And anything harmful to the individual is actually detrimental to society as a whole.

෬ **27** ෨

PROSPEROUS PEOPLE ARE NOT FIXATED WITH DISCOUNTS, COUPONS AND SALES.

Prosperous people are never afraid to purchase things at a fair exchange of value. They don't pass up savings when offered, but that is not the sole basis upon which they make their buying decision.

Rather than exerting undue effort in negotiating tactics, coupon searching, or trying for an advantage, they would rather spend their time creating more value, which manifests as greater prosperity.

∝ **28** ∞

THERE IS NO PLACE ON EARTH THAT PROSPERITY IS NOT.

People see pockets of poverty like famines and ghettos and think that prosperity is absent there, but such is not the case. Prosperity is in the ethers, surrounding us everywhere, even in places where lack seems apparent. It is not that prosperity isn't there; it is that man is not manifesting it.

Primitives thought that the sun deserted the earth every night. In actuality, the earth turns away from the sun. It is the same way with prosperity. It never leaves us, but we sometimes turn away from it.

෬ **29** ෭

MANIFESTING PROSPERITY IS NOT ABOUT JUDGMENT.

An opposite but equal force balances everything in the universe. Masculine and feminine, yin and yang, positive and negative. All just transactions are based upon the principle of win-win, or put another way, fair exchange of values.

Now I should interject here that I use the term negative for purposes of clarity of illustration. In actuality, I believe that the force that created the world is positive and good. The things we may label negative and bad are caused not by a "bad" God or universe, but by our reactions to that good.

If you get a flat tire on your way to the supermarket, you probably think that is bad. But the guy who owns the tire store (who is trying to send his daughter to college) might see it as good.

I could choose to think that my teeth alignment was negative. But my dentist who did my braces may have another viewpoint.

Winter is not bad and summer is not good. And spring does not have to be bad for fall to be good. They just are. And we need the contrasts for anything to have meaning for us. So, the point here is not to philosophize about what is good or bad, or get sidetracked by labels. The important thing is that you realize that nothing is free; everything comes at a fair exchange of value.

Everything.

❧ **30** ❧

YOUR ASSOCIATION WITH MONEY DETERMINES WHETHER YOU ATTRACT IT OR NOT.

Broke people usually have a negative energy and connotation surrounding money. They obsess about how they are unable to do things that require money.

Wealthy people have a very positive association with money. They view it in terms of the freedom, enjoyment and pleasure it brings them.

Having a negative association of money repels it from you, while a positive association attracts it to you.

≪ 31 ≫

YOU WON'T GET YOUR NEXT ASSIGNMENT, UNTIL YOU'VE FINISHED YOUR CURRENT ONE.

And not just finished it, but also done it correctly, to the best of your ability. A life of prosperity is a series of assignments, each one growing you, developing your talents, and expanding your consciousness. As your consciousness grows, so does the impact you make. So your responsibilities increase, as your ability to meet them increases. You start to influence a bigger circle, which attracts greater prosperity to you.

∝ **32** ∾

PROSPERITY CONSCIOUS PEOPLE ARE CONTRARIANS.

Unfortunately, most of the masses are sick, broke and unhappy, eking out their lives of quiet desperation. They drudge through each day, doing what they are told, and what they are expected to do. They don't know how to think. They have been told WHAT to think for so long, that they no longer know HOW to think. If you want to succeed —you need to be a contrarian.

But to do this, you must be capable of critical thought. Which is something the herd cannot yet do. The reason most people are living those desperate lives is that they are incapable of discernment. The reason Bill Gates is a billionaire is that he can discern things that others can't.

Question what you read and hear. Analyze why the herd thinks the way it does.

And think differently!

⚝ 33 ⚝

YOUR WEALTH WILL GROW ONLY AS FAST AS YOU DO.

As you grow, your consciousness develops. As your consciousness grows, you attract more prosperity to you. There are no shortcuts here. You must be willing to do the personal development necessary to become the person who is trusted and blessed with great prosperity.

C8 34 ෨

THE UNIVERSE CAN ONLY DO FOR YOU, WHAT CAN BE DONE THROUGH YOU.

The Quakers like to say, "As you pray, move your feet." The universe makes the light available to you, but you still must turn on the light switch. Planning prosperity is good, but it is still just planning. Once you have your affirmations planned, create your action plan.

‹ 35 ›

GOSSIPING ABOUT OTHERS CREATES A NEGATIVE PROSPERITY DEBT.

This is an offshoot of the vacuum law of prosperity. When you gossip about others, you are a voyeur to their discomfort, and incur a karma debt for this. This also holds true when you watch "reality" television shows that exploit people's ignorance for the entertainment of the public.

ඥ **36** ෨

WHEN REVENGE WALKS OUT— PROSPERITY WALKS IN.

One of the biggest blocks toward prosperity comes from people holding on to resentment, revenge, and hurt. Prosperity cannot exist in a heart that is holding these things. Hanging on to these emotions hurts only the person holding them, and keeps prosperity at bay.

You must forgive all those who have wronged you in life. And you must especially forgive one more person. Yourself. If you cannot forgive yourself, you cannot accept abundance.

෨ **37** ෫

YOUR DREAM HAS NEVER BEEN CLOSER THAN IT IS AT THIS EXACT INSTANT!

There are no coincidences in life, and it is no accident that you have discovered this prosperity book series. You are a person of vision, or you wouldn't have gotten this far. You have educated yourself on how prosperity laws work. You know that a person with a compelling dream actually bends the Universe to their will.

Manifesting abundant prosperity comes from learning the secrets that govern it. Which you have just done. Go for it!

About Randy Gage

For more than 15 years, Randy Gage has been helping people transform self-limiting beliefs into self-fulfilling breakthroughs to achieve their dreams. Randy's story of rising from a jail cell as a teen, to a self-made millionaire, has inspired millions around the world.

This compelling journey of triumph over fear, self-doubt, and addiction, uniquely qualifies him as an undisputed expert in the arena of peak performance and extraordinary human achievement. His story and the way he shares it, demonstrate the true power of the mind over outside circumstances.

Randy Gage is a modern-day explorer in the field of body-mind development and personal growth. He is the author of many best-selling albums including, *Dynamic Development* and *Prosperity* and is the director of www.BreakthroughU.com.

People from around the world interact and receive personal coaching from Randy through "Breakthrough U," his online coaching and success program. As Dean of BreakthroughU.com, Randy provides insight into how to overcome fear, doubt and self-sabotage to reach success and achieve the highest level of human potential.

For more resources and to subscribe to Randy's free ezine newsletters, visit www.RandyGage.com.

101 Keys to Your Prosperity

"Insights on health, happiness and abundance in your life."

You are meant to be healthy, happy and prosperous. Once you recognize and accept this, it is simply a case of learning the principles that abundance is based on.

In this insightful book, Randy Gage reveals 101 keys to manifesting that prosperity in your own life. You will move from lack consciousness to living in the light of true abundance. You'll discover:

- What creates prosperity consciousness;
- The universal laws that govern prosperity;
- Why you should embrace critical thinking;
- The secret of creating a vacuum for good; and,
- What it takes to manifest prosperity on the physical plane.

**Order the print book or downloadable eBook online at
www.Prosperity-Insights.com**

Quantity pricing for paperback book:

1–9 books	$7.00 each
10–99 books	$6.00 each
100–499 books	$5.00 each
500–999 books	$4.00 each
1,000 + books	$3.00 each

Accept Your Abundance!
Why You are Supposed to Be Wealthy

"Claim the Prosperity that is your Birthright."

Do you believe that it is somehow spiritual to be poor? One reading of this fascinating book will dissuade you of that belief fast. You'll understand that you are meant to be healthy, happy and wealthy.

Prosperity guru Randy Gage cuts through the religious dogmas to reveal why becoming rich is your spiritual destiny. You'll discover:

- Why poverty is a sin;
- What may be keeping you from your prosperity;
- Why being wealthy is your natural state;
- The difference between the way rich and poor people think; and,
- How to attract and accept your true abundance!

**Order the print book or downloadable eBook online at
www.Prosperity-Insights.com**

Quantity pricing for paperback book:

1–9 books	$7.00 each
10–99 books	$6.00 each
100–499 books	$5.00 each
500–999 books	$4.00 each
1,000 + books	$3.00 each

Order Online at **www.Prosperity-Insights.com**
or call 1-800-432-4243 or (316) 942-1111

37 Secrets About Prosperity

"A revealing look at how you manifest wealth."

In this landmark book, prosperity guru Randy Gage unveils 37 little-known insights into the science of prosperity. Gage breaks it down into simple, understandable explanations, so you can apply the information in your life immediately to create your own prosperity. He reveals how he went from a dishwasher in a pancake house to a self-made multi-millionaire.

You'll learn:

- Why most people remain poor;
- How the rich leverage their prosperity;
- Why you should emulate certain business models;
- What separates broke, sick and unhappy people from the rich, healthy and happy ones; and,
- How you can manifest prosperity in all areas of your life.

Order the print book or downloadable eBook online at www.Prosperity-Insights.com

Quantity pricing for paperback book:

1–9 books	$7.00 each
10–99 books	$6.00 each
100–499 books	$5.00 each
500–999 books	$4.00 each
1,000 + books	$3.00 each

Prosperity Mind!
How to Harness the Power of Thought

*"Brilliant Insights on health, happiness
and abundance in your life."*

Since "Think and Grow Rich,"
people have been fascinated with
the power of the mind to accomplish
great things. Now a recognized
expert in human potential cracks
the code on how you program
yourself for prosperity!

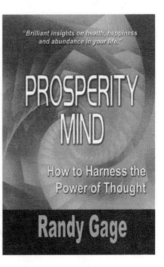

In this breakthrough book,
prosperity guru Randy Gage reveals
how you can actually program your
subconscious mind to move from
lack consciousness to prosperity
thought. In it, you'll discover:

- How to identify self-limiting
  beliefs that hold you back;
- The 5 common
  expressions you probably use every day, which
  program you for failure on a subconscious level;
- How to practice the "vacuum law" of prosperity to
  attract good in your life;
- Imaging techniques to manifest things you want;
  and,
- How you can actually program your own
  subconscious mind for riches!

**Order the print book or downloadable eBook online at
www.Prosperity-Insights.com**

Quantity pricing for paperback book:

1–9 books	$7.00 each
10–99 books	$6.00 each
100–499 books	$5.00 each
500–999 books	$4.00 each
1,000 + books	$3.00 each

The 7 Spiritual Laws of Prosperity

"Live your life by the universal laws that govern health, happiness and abundance."

It is your birthright to be healthy, happy and prosperous. Accept this truth and it's simply a case of learning and living by the 7 Spiritual Laws that govern abundance.

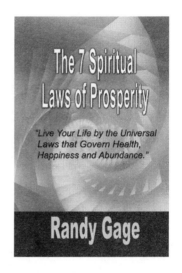

In this breakthrough and insightful book, Randy Gage reveals the secrets behind harnessing these laws to manifest your own prosperity. You'll learn about each of these Prosperity Laws and discover how to:

- Create a vacuum for good;
- Use imaging to get what you want;
- Find and keep your perfect soul mate;
- Use creativity to get the bills paid; and,
- Attract money, health and harmony to your life.

Order the print book or downloadable eBook online at www.Prosperity-Insights.com

Quantity pricing for paperback book:

1–9 books	$7.00 each
10–99 books	$6.00 each
100–499 books	$5.00 each
500–999 books	$4.00 each
1,000 + books	$3.00 each

The Prosperity Series
by Randy Gage

You are meant to be healthy, happy and prosperous. Once you recognize and accept this, it is simply a case of learning the principles that abundance is based on.

In this insightful series, you will move from lack consciousness to living in the light of true abundance.

Randy Gage reveals . . .
- What creates prosperity consciousness;
- The universal laws that govern prosperity;
- Why you should embrace critical thinking;
- The secret to creating a vacuum for good;
- What it takes to manifest prosperity on the physical plane; and,
- Why you are supposed to be wealthy.

Get all five books now and start living a life of abundance!

OrderThe Prosperity Series by Randy Gage online:
www.Prosperity-Insights.com

The Prosperity Series, 5 print books $30
The Prosperity Series, 5 eBooks $20
The Prosperity Series, all 5 print books and eBooks
Combination Special $47

Prosperity:
How to Apply Spiritual Laws to Create Health, Wealth and Abundance in Your Life
by Randy Gage

This album will help you uncover the subconscious "lack" programming you have that is holding you back. Then, you'll replace it with prosperity consciousness to manifest money, health, great relationships, happiness, and strong spiritual harmony.

True prosperity comes from understanding and living by the spiritual laws that govern our world. This album takes you through each of the Seven Spiritual Laws that govern prosperity—and shows you how to apply them. You will discover the ancient secrets to manifest prosperity in your own life.

You'll discover:
- Why you're supposed to be rich;
- The secrets of optimum health;
- How to get out of debt;
- The Seven Spiritual Laws you must live by;
- Your special powers for prosperity; and,
- How to image—then manifest—boundless, limitless prosperity.

This album will take you on a journey of spiritual enlightenment. You'll learn the practical applications so you can manifest prosperity in your life NOW! Y ou'll learn about faith, the principle of attraction, and even how to use creativity to get the bills paid! This is the most specific, detailed and comprehensive album ever produced on how to become prosperous. **D on't you need it now?**

Prosperity: 8 CDs #A28CD $107
Prosperity: 8 audio-tape album #A28 $97

Dynamic Development
**Achieve Your True Potential with the Dynamic Development Series
by Randy Gage**

Do you live a life of joy—or simply get through the week? Can you communicate well with your family and co-workers, or do you struggle to be heard? Are you in open, honest and loving relationships, or do you hide behind a mask? <u>How much more can you earn, learn, love and accomplish</u>? *If you want to break out of self-imposed limitations and break through to your true potential—the* **Dynamic Development Series** *is the perfect resource for you.*

Instantly hailed when it was released as the ultimate self-development resource, this is a two-year program to nurture your personal growth and achieve your innate greatness. Each month you will receive an audiotape from human achievement expert Randy Gage with a lesson, and some "homework" to complete that month.

It's a continuing journey on your path of personal development. Each month will bring you on an in-depth study in some area of human achievement, whether body, mind or soul. You'll discover new truths about yourself and uncover old ones. You'll desire more, obtain more, and accomplish more . . . by becoming more.

Dynamic Development, Volume 1, 12 audio-tapes
#V2 $147

Dynamic Development, Volume2, 12 audio-tapes
V4 $147

BEST DEAL! Both Dynamic Development Volumes,
24 audio-tapes #V2V4S $247

Crafting Your Vision

Twelve success experts share their secrets to success . . .

As soon as this 12 audio-tape album was released, it was hailed as one of the greatest self-development tools since *Think and Grow Rich!* I t gets to the real root cause of success or failure—the vision you create for yourself.

It's pleasing to your ego to assume your prosperity is not growing because of outside factors and other circumstances. **But the truth is—you are reaping the results of the vision you created!**

Your suffering, frustration or failure to reach goals is the result of a neutral or negative vision— just as the blessings in your life are the results of a positive vision. This is an immutable, unshakable universal law. Living the lifestyle of your dreams begins with crafting the vision of where you want to go. For without a clear, compelling vision you simply cannot achieve what you're truly capable of. And there simply is no better resource to help you create an empowering vision for yourself than this amazing resource.

You'll learn how to craft your personal vision, how to design a vision big enough to encompass the visions of your people, and the steps to take on a daily basis to bring your vision to reality. You'll hear 12 complete programs on vision—recorded live—from 12 of the foremost experts on direct selling, recruiting and marketing.

This breakthrough album includes talks by:

Richard Brooke	Michael S. Clouse	Rita Davenport
John Milton Fogg	Matthew Freese	Randy Gage
Lisa Jimenez, M.Ed.	John Kalench	John David Mann
Jan Ruhe	Tom Schreiter	Tom Welch

When you finish, you'll really know how to craft and manifest the vision of where you want to go. Make sure this resource is in your personal development library. **Get it today!**

Crafting Your Vision: 12 audio-tape album #A30 $97

Get Randy Gage As

The only ongoing education program specifically designed for your success! Get personal, individualized success coaching from **Randy Gage**. Join Randy as he helps you expand your vision, shatter self-doubt, and reach your true success potential. Breakthrough U is your opportunity to have Randy as your personal success coach— mentoring you through the mindset, consciousness, and daily actions necessary to reach the success you are capable of.

Initiate Level

This is level one of an amazing journey of self-discovery. Each day you will receive a "Daily Awakening" e-mail message filled with mind-expanding exercises and success lessons to teach you how to think like ultra-successful people think. In addition to these "mind aerobics," you'll receive marketing tips, prosperity secrets and just general success information on how to make it to the top.

You will also have access to the members-only forum on the site so that you can network with other success-minded individuals, and get an invitation to attend Randy's BreakthroughU Success Events.

This is priced inexpensively and is for the beginning success seeker. If you've faced adversity, are deeply in debt, maxed out on your credit cards, or simply starting the journey—this is the program for you. Randy created this level so that those who are down and out— but committed to getting "up and in" — have a vehicle to do so. It's a program to change your consciousness, one day at a time.

Now, if you are further along the path, and serious about reaching higher levels of success—you're ready to advance to...

Alchemist Level

Alchemy, if you'll remember, is the medieval philosophy of transmutation: converting base metals to gold. This is the level for you if you're seeking a transmutation in your life: converting base thoughts and desires into the thinking and actions that produce rich and prosperous outcomes.

(continued on the next page)

Order Online at **www.RandyGage.com**
or call 1-800-432-4243 or (316) 942-1111

Your Personal Coach!

Like the Initiate Level, you will receive the Daily Awakening messages, access to the members-only forum, and an invitation to Randy's Success Convention. You will also receive:

- The "Alchemy Transmutation Kit" (with intro lesson, CDs and binder);
- Subscription to the monthly lessons;
- Access to the monthly online video seminars;
- Monthly Tele-seminars
- Two Personalized Consultations

Now, if you're serious as a heart attack about success, and want to get even more individualized and personal coaching...you might want to consider the pinnacle level:

Mastermind Council

This is Randy's "inner circle" of select consulting clients, business partners, and colleagues. They receive a package of benefits so lucrative, that it's never been offered anywhere before. Membership in the **Mastermind Council** gives you a chance to get the most personalized help and guidance from me individually— as well as interacting with some of the brightest entrepreneurial minds on the planet.

In addition to the same benefits as the Alchemist, you will also receive:

- Ten Personalized Consultations;
- The chance to participate in twelve live Mastermind Conference Calls a year;
- Members-only Council Updates; and,
- The chance to participate in the Mastermind Retreats each year.

For complete details go to:
www.BreakthroughU.com
Randy Gage's
BREAKTHROUGHU™

The Midas Mentality:
Expecting and Accepting Your Abundance

This program is the first resource of its kind, ever developed in the world. It will transform you from lack and limitation programming to prosperity consciousness. For 31 days, Randy Gage will work with you, helping you go through the same transformation that he did. He will help you peel away limiting beliefs and replace them with beliefs that serve you and he will help you identify fears and conquer them.

And level upon level, he will guide you in a metamorphosis of your thought process—from how sick, unhappy and broke people think—to the way healthy, happy, rich people do.

30 Audio CDs, 2 DVDs, Study Guide & Randy Jr. CDRom

It is a multi-media format, scientifically developed to literally change the way you think. You will create new neural pathways in your brain, develop your critical thinking skills, and foster whole brain synchronicity between the two hemispheres of your brain.

You will develop the multi-millionaire's mindset, which is the first—and most critical—step to becoming open.

On day one, you'll watch the DVD entitled, "The Science of Manifesting Prosperity." Then you'll load the CD-ROM into your computer. This will cause the "Randy Jr" character to pop up on your computer screen once each day, giving you one of his 101 keys to prosperity.

Then on the next day, you'll start the first of 30 daily lessons on audio CD. You listen to each lesson, then go to your workbook and complete the day's task. On average, this will take you from 45 minutes an hour per day. Do only one lesson each day, to ensure that it "sets," and you are at a different consciousness when you start the next day's lesson.

Following the thirty CDs and workbook lessons, you then watch the final DVD, "Putting Your Prosperity in Place." Of course the "Randy Jr." character will keep popping up everyday, to keep your thoughts on track.

Trust me when I tell you that you will be thinking entirely different than when you started. You will have the mindset of a multi-millionaire, the single most important step to becoming one. You see, you can't be treated for prosperity; you can only be open to receiving it. By the time you finish this program, you will be. Really.

The Midas Mentality–30 audio CDs, 2 DVDs, Study Guide & Randy Jr. CDRom $997

Order Online at **www.ProsperityUniverse.com**
or call 1-800-432-4243 or (316) 942-1111

Randy Gage's Recommended Resources	Price	Qty	Total
Prosperity by Randy Gage Select: ¨ audiotapes or ¨ CD's	$97 (tapes) $107 (CDs)		
The Midas Mentality 30 day prosperity program	$997		
Dynamic Development Series Volume One by Randy Gage	$147		
Crafting Your Vision 12 audiotape album	$97		
Prosperity Series 5 books	$30		
101 Keys to Your Prosperity book	$7		
The 7 Spiritual Laws of Prosperity book	$7		
Prosperity Mind! book	$7		
Accept Your Abundance! book	$7		
37 Secrets About Prosperity book	$7		

United Parcel Shipping Table Order Total 2-Day Ground $50.00 or under $11.60 $5.50 $50.01-$250.00 $13.20 $6.00 $250.01-over $16.20 $7.00 For Alaska, Hawaii, and Canada - regular shipping cost, and add 10%. For foreign and overseas orders, figure the total of your order, plus the regular shipping cost, and add 20%	Subtotal $_____ Shipping (see chart) $_____
Terms: 60-day money back guarantee! Contact us within 60 days of your invoice date if, for any reason, you're not 100% satisfied with any product you've received from us. Product must be in re-sellable condition. Customer Service: 1-800-946-7804 or (316) 942-1111	$_____ **TOTAL**

PAYMENT TYPE: ¨ **Visa** ¨ **MC** ¨ **AMEX** ¨ **Discover** or ¨ **Cash** ¨ **Check**

Please print clearly
Credit Card # _ _ _ _ _ _ _ _ _ _ _ _ _ _ _ _

Expires: (MM/YY) ____/____ Signature:_____

Full Name:

Address: Apt./Suite#

City: State: Zip: Country:

Phone: Email:

Ordering & Customer Service: Prime Concepts Group Inc.
1807 S. Eisenhower St. • Wichita, Kansas 67209-2810 USA
1-800-432-4243 or (316) 942-1111 • Fax: (316) 942-5313
www.ProsperityUniverse.com